Cursive

THE
Rhythm
OF HANDWRITING

DENISE EIDE

Logic of English

The Rhythm of Handwriting Cursive Student Book

Logic of English® is a Registered Trademark of Logic of English, Inc
Printed in the United States of America

Logic of English, Inc
4865 19th Street NW, Suite 130
Rochester, MN 55901

Cover Design: Dugan Design Group
LOE School Font: David Occhino Design

ISBN: 978-1-936706-70-9

Second Edition

20 19 18 17 16 15 14 13 12

www.logicofenglish.com

TABLE OF CONTENTS

INTRODUCTION

Research has shown that students who write fluently and legibly have:

1. A clear understanding of how each letter is formed.

2. Rhythmic handwriting which pauses only at the natural stopping points.

3. Automatic muscle memory for each letter.

The explicit instruction and rhythmic language in *The Rhythm of Handwriting Series* aids students with each of these points, fostering the development of beautiful and consistent handwriting.

In order to most efficiently develop muscle memory, letters are organized by their initial strokes, rather than alphabetically.

Before beginning, introduce the lines using the Handwriting Chart on page 17 or the *Logic of English Whiteboard*. Show the students the baseline, top line, and midline. Ask the students to repeat back the name of each line.

Teachers may choose whether or not to teach the strokes needed to form each letter. Some students benefit from isolated stroke instruction, whereas other students prefer to see how all the pieces fit together. The strokes needed for each letter are listed at the beginning of each section.

STEPS TO TEACHING HANDWRITING

1. Show the students the *Phonogram Flash Card* for the targeted letter. Say the sound(s) found on the back of the flashcard.

2. Ask the students to repeat the sound(s). (Correct errors in pronunciation.)

3. Show the students the targeted letter in the workbook. Discuss how the cursive letter is the same as or different from the bookface form. Point out the connector strokes and how they make it easier to write the letter and connect it to other letters.

4. Using your pointer finger, demonstrate how to write the letter while saying the full directions aloud, followed by the sounds of the phonogram. (For many students, it is beneficial to teach step one, ask the students to demonstrate, then reteach step one and add step two, ask the students to demonstrate, etc.)

5. Ask the students to write the letter with their pointer fingers while saying the full directions aloud followed by the sounds.

6. Model writing the letter using the shortened, bold instructions. Emphasize the rhythm. End by saying the sound(s) made by the letter.

7. Ask the students to model correct formation 3-5 times with their pointer fingers while repeating the rhythmic directions, followed by the letter's sound(s). Check that the students are developing fluid and rhythmic motions.

8. **Optional:** Direct the students to trace the enlarged letter in the workbook with their pointer fingers, or practice with the *Rhythm of Handwriting Tactile Cards.*

STUDENTS WITH WEAK FINE-MOTOR SKILLS

9. Practice the letters using large-motor motions on the *Logic of English Whiteboard*, a chalkboard, or in a sensory box. Continue to develop fine-motor skills by coloring, stringing beads, playing with building toys, and other activities. When the students' motor skills have developed, move on to Step 10.

STUDENTS WITH STRONG FINE-MOTOR SKILLS

10. Practice writing the letter with a pencil. Allow students to choose the line size that is most comfortable for their hands.

HANDWRITING TIPS

TEACH LOWERCASE LETTERS FIRST

Lowercase letters comprise more than 90% of all that we read and write. Uppercase letters are used only at the beginning of sentences and with proper nouns. Teaching lowercase letters first provides students with the most vital information they need to be successful in writing. Once students have mastered the lowercase letters, they should be taught how to write the capital letters and when they are used.

TEACH HANDWRITING USING ALL FOUR LEARNING MODES

When teaching students how to write, always use all four learning modalities: seeing, hearing, doing, and speaking. Show the students how to form the letter (seeing) while providing explicit spoken directions (hearing). Then ask the students to repeat the action (doing) while repeating the directions aloud (speaking).

TEACH EACH LETTER WITH LARGE–MOTOR MOVEMENTS

Teach letter formation using large muscle movements originating from the elbow. Demonstrate the motions using your pointer finger on the large handwriting charts or the *Logic of English Whiteboard*. Students should then imitate the motions using their pointer fingers and movements that originate from the elbow. Once the motions have been learned, students should practice the sequence of movements writing with a marker on the *Logic of English Whiteboard*, on a chalkboard, in the air, in sensory boxes, with sandpaper letters, or with tactile letters.

PROVIDE CLEAR AND EXPLICIT DIRECTIONS

Some students who have poor handwriting are unclear about how to form the letters and how they relate to the lines on the page. When teaching, it is important to provide students with full, explicit directions on letter formation, leaving no room for confusion. *The Rhythm of Handwriting Series* includes explicit directions for introducing each letter. Students who are sensitive to too much auditory input may learn each letter using only the rhythmic, bold instructions.

EMPHASIZE THE RHYTHM OF HANDWRITING

Fluent handwriting is rhythmic, pausing only at the natural stopping or reversal points in the letters. Other than the natural stopping points, the pencil should continue in a steady motion. The bold keywords in *The Rhythm of Handwriting* materials provide students with abbreviated directions which accent the natural rhythm of each letter.

STROKES OR NO STROKES?

Some students benefit greatly by learning the strokes in isolation before learning how to write each letter. These students see each letter as a puzzle that is formed by putting the pieces of the strokes together. Other students feel confused by learning the strokes in isolation and have the greatest success by learning how to write each letter as a whole. Experiment to find your student's learning style by teaching the relevant strokes before teaching a letter. Practice writing the strokes with the pointer finger on the handwriting chart provided. Ask the student if it was helpful. If the student finds this helpful, continue in the same manner with the following chapters. If the student was confused by learning the strokes individually, then skip the strokes page and move straight into teaching the letters.

CROSSING T'S AND F'S

Students should cross the lowercase "t" and "f" in the direction of reading and writing, i.e. from left to right. In cursive, write the whole word before picking up the pencil to cross or dot a letter.

PROVIDE SUPPORT

Until students have mastered how to form the letters with ease, they should not practice alone. Students who are asked to copy letters without direct instruction tend to focus on the visual image rather than the motions needed to write the letter. This detracts from building the muscle memory needed to write fluidly. In addition, without clear instruction, some students will reverse the image, making it more likely for them to struggle with reversals in both handwriting and reading. Clear, explicit teaching using all the learning modalities will eliminate confusion and reversals.

In addition, careful guidance from the beginning will prevent bad habits from forming. Investing time now to ensure that each student develops correct muscle memory for each letter and understands how each letter is formed will save you much time and frustration in the future for both writing and reading.

LIMIT COPYWORK UNTIL THE STUDENT CAN READ

Students should not be asked to copy letters, words, sentences, or paragraphs until they are able to read the sounds and words they are copying. When asked to do so sooner, the task is akin to art, and void of any language learning value.

Once students have mastered writing and reading several of the single-letter phonograms, they may begin to combine the single-letter phonograms into words. When students begin to write words in *The Rhythm of Handwriting Series*, they should read the word aloud and then write the word, saying the sound of each letter while they write.

ENCOURAGE MASTERY

It is only through abundant practice that students learn to write fluently. Require daily handwriting practice until all the letters have been mastered. At the end of a practice session, ask the students to evaluate their own writing by picking the letter or word on the page that is written the most neatly. Ask the student to explain why it is the best. Then, as the teacher, choose the letter that you think is written the most neatly and explain why.

For some students a letter may need to be retaught a second or even third day before all motions are mastered. This is particularly true after a weekend or break. Simply repeat the steps. Always provide clear, explicit instruction. Require students to model the motions correctly while repeating the directions aloud.

TRANSITIONING TO PENCIL AND PAPER

The decision to transition to pencil and paper should be based upon the age, development, and prior experiences of the student. Many older students will find great success in learning to write a letter using large-motor motions with the handwriting chart, then immediately writing the letter with a pencil.

Students with less developed fine-motor skills benefit from extended large-motor practice. By learning letter formation with movements that originate from the elbow as opposed to the fingers, students are programming the motions and rhythms into their brains. The muscle memory which is formed using large-motor movements will translate into fine-motor motions once the student has developed fine-motor skills. If a student is lagging with fine-motor development, writing exercises may continue with large-motor practice using a whiteboard, chalkboard, sandpaper letters, tactile letters, and sensory boxes until his fine-motor development is sufficient for writing with a pencil.

During this time students should also be engaged in fine-motor activities on a daily basis. Many of the examples below require adult supervision.

- Color with markers, chalk, crayons, and other media.
- Provide an eyedropper and small paper cups. Fill one cup with water. Direct students to transfer the water with the eyedropper. For added fun, use a few drops of food coloring in each cup and allow students to experiment with mixing colors.
- Make necklaces and bracelets with plastic beads.
- Use tweezers to move beads from one cup to another.
- Provide students with small colored pom-poms and direct them to sort them by color.
- Provide clothespins that pinch. String a rope between two chairs and allow students to hang up doll clothes, socks, or pictures to display.
- Use child-safe scissors.
- Provide students with bolts, nuts, and washers of varying sizes to sort and screw together.
- Play with building toys.

Many students will benefit from some or all of the following tips when transitioning from large-motor movements to writing on paper. Clear and explicit teaching can prevent unnecessary confusion and provide students with the support they need to succeed.

PENCIL GRIP

Instruct the students how to hold the pencil with the thumb and the first finger so the pencil rests gently on the middle finger. If the student struggles to hold the pencil correctly, provide a pencil grip.

PAPER POSITION

Demonstrate how to place the paper at an angle so the arm naturally sweeps from the elbow rather than needing to tense the shoulder or twist the wrist. Ask the students to make curved sweeping lines along the paper, using motions from their elbow. Then position the paper so the student's strokes follow the lines of the paper.

LINE SIZE

The Rhythm of Handwriting Cursive Student Book provides a variety of line sizes for each exercise. Allow the student to experiment. Discuss: which line is the most comfortable? On which size does the student write the most neatly? Which line size is a better fit for the student's hand? In future exercises allow the student to choose the line size that is most comfortable and results in the most legible writing.

Despite conventional wisdom that young students should use paper with giant spaces between the lines, many beginning writers benefit from much smaller lines. Because they have small hands, smaller lines encourage students to use fine-motor movements originating in the fingers without stretching uncomfortably.

SUGGESTED SCHEDULES

STUDENTS AGES SIX AND UNDER

Students six and under should learn one letter per day. Each lesson should include:
- Introduction to a new letter, including its sound(s) and how to write it.
- Practice matching sounds to previously learned letters.
- Practice reading previously learned letters.
- Practice writing previously learned letters.

Logic of English, Inc publishes *The Phonogram and Spelling Game Book,* which may be used to enhance review.

STUDENTS AGES SEVEN AND UP

SCHEDULE 1

Learn two letters per day starting with the lowercase letters.

SCHEDULE 2

Learn four letters per day starting with the lowercase letters.

SCHEDULE 3

Each day, learn all the letters based upon one initial stroke. Begin with the lowercase swing letters.

Ideas For Handwriting Practice

LETTER DICTATION

Provide students with a whiteboard, chalkboard, sensory box, or paper. Say the sound(s) of one of the letters. Direct the students to write the letter.

BLIND WRITING

Direct the students to close their eyes and write the letter five to ten times without looking. Without visual cues, the students must rely on muscle memory. Instruct the students to open their eyes and choose the letter that is written the most legibly.

SPEED WRITING

Set a timer for 20 seconds. Direct students to write the letter as many times as possible before the timer beeps. Instruct the students to choose the letter that is written most legibly.

TREASURE HUNT

Hide the *Rhythm of Handwriting Tactile Cards* around the room. Direct students to find the letters and bring them back to you. When they find a letter they must read the sound(s) and demonstrate how to write it.

LETTER STATIONS

Set up stations of whiteboards, chalkboards, or sensory boxes around the room. Students will rotate between the stations. Call out the sound(s) of a letter. The students must write the letter at their station. Every two to three letters, rotate to the next station.

SKY WRITING

Call out the sound(s) of a letter. Direct students to write it in the air using their arm and pointer finger.

SIMON SAYS

Appoint one student to be "Simon." Provide the student with a set of flash cards containing all the letters that have been learned. "Simon" draws a card and reads the sound(s). The other students must write the letter on small whiteboards.

FOOT WRITING

Direct students to lie on their backs on the floor. Call out the sound(s) made by one of the letters. Direct students to write the letter in the air using their foot.

WRITING GAME

Direct two students to sit back to back. Each person will need a small whiteboard. The first person writes a letter on the whiteboard, then tells the other person the directions for writing the letter. The other person then writes the letter. If both people have written the same letter they get one point.

Lowercase

Cursive LETTERS

Handwriting Chart

Identify the baseline, midline, and top line.

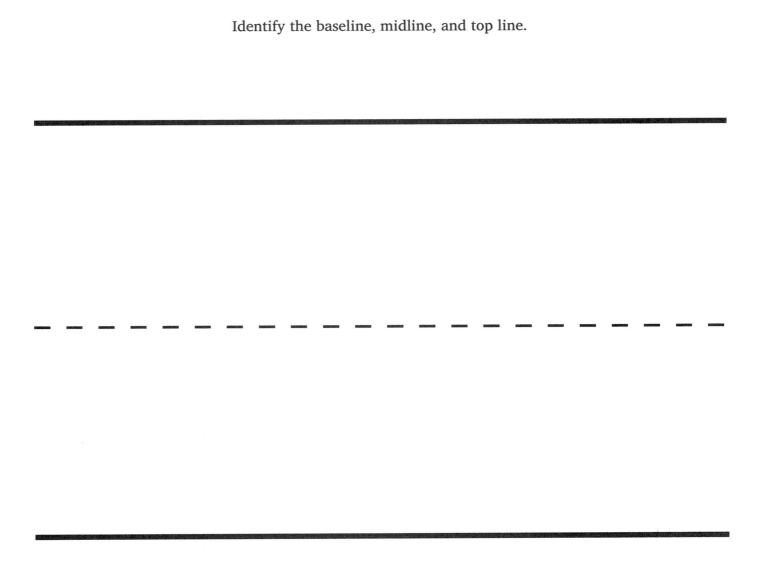

SWING LETTERS

Each of the lowercase swing letters begins on the baseline with an upward swinging motion toward the midline.

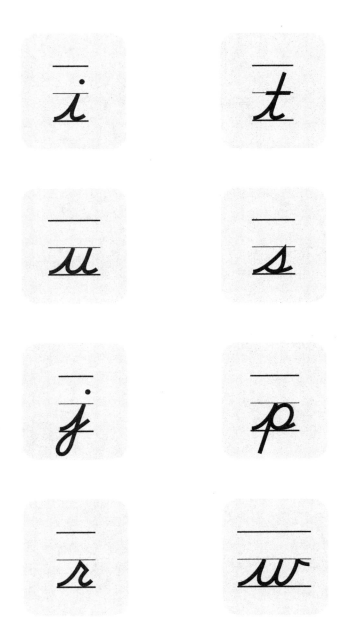

STROKES

SWING

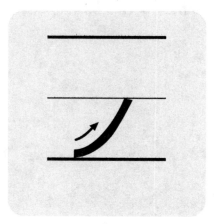

DOWN

CIRCLE

GLIDE

DROP-SWOOP

SCOOP

DIP

CROSS

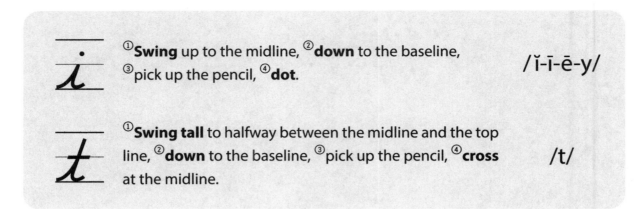

①**Swing** up to the midline, ②**down** to the baseline, ③pick up the pencil, ④**dot**.   /ĭ-ī-ē-y/

①**Swing tall** to halfway between the midline and the top line, ②**down** to the baseline, ③pick up the pencil, ④**cross** at the midline.   /t/

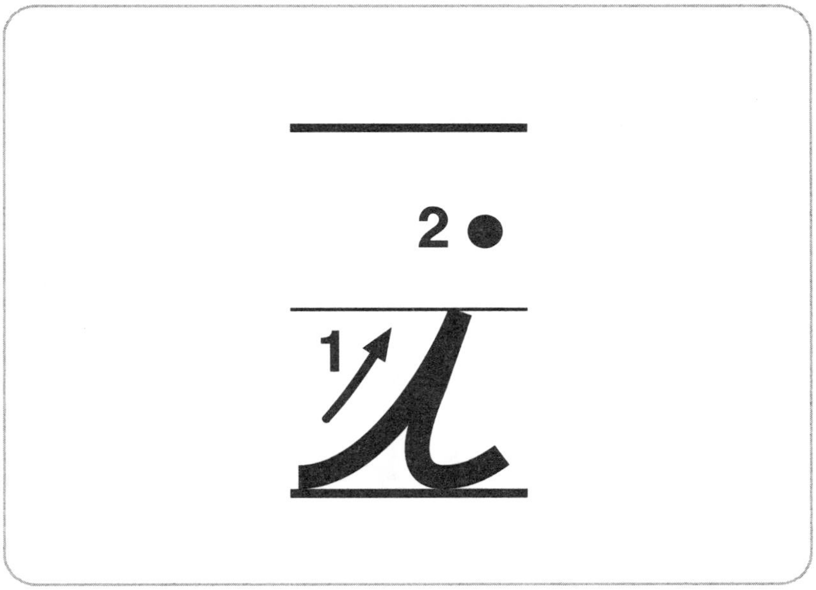

i

i

i

i i i i i i i i i i i i i i i i i i i

i i i i i i i i i i i i i i i i i ii

i

i

i

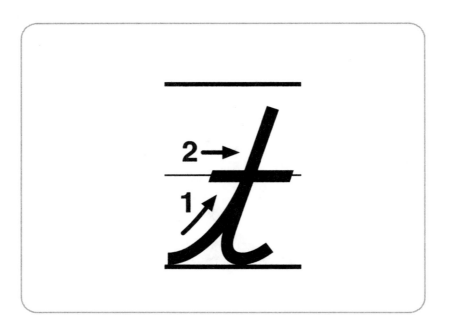

t

t t t t t t t t t t t t t t t t t t t t t t t t t t t

t t t t t t t t t t t t t t t t t t t

t

t

t

t

t

u ①**Swing** up to the midline, ②**down** to the baseline, ③**swing** up to the midline, ④**down** to the baseline.   /ŭ-ū-ö-ü/

s ①**Swing** up to the midline, ②**scoop** around, ③touch, ④**glide**.   /s-z/

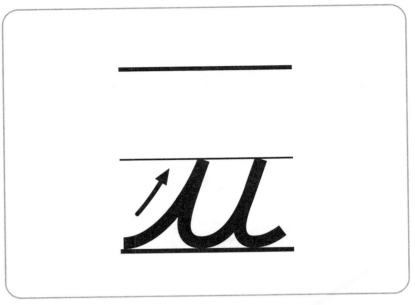

𝓊 𝓊 𝓊 𝓊 𝓊 𝓊 𝓊 𝓊 𝓊 𝓊 𝓊 𝓊 𝓊 𝓊 𝓊 𝓊

𝓊 𝓊 𝓊 𝓊 𝓊 𝓊 𝓊 𝓊 𝓊 𝓊 𝓊 𝓊 𝓊 𝓊 𝓊

𝓊

𝓊

𝓊

𝓊

𝓊

𝓊

①**Swing** up to the midline, ②**drop** down halfway below the baseline, ③**swoop**, ④pick up the pencil, ⑤**dot**.   /j/

①**Swing** up to the midline, ②**drop** down halfway below the baseline, ③slide **up** to the midline, ④**circle** around to the baseline, ⑤touch, ⑥**glide**.   /p/

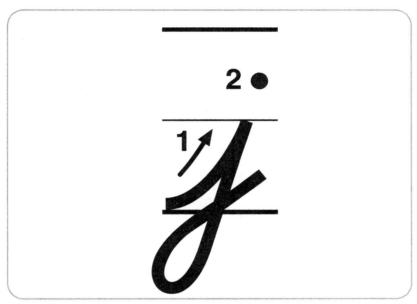

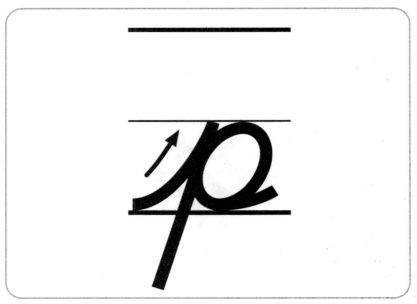

p p p p p p p p p p p p p p p p p p p p p p p

p p p p p p p p p p p p p p p p p p p p p p p

p

p

p

p

p

p

①**Swing** up to the midline, ②**dip**, ③**down** to the baseline. /r/

①**Swing** up to the midline, ②**down** to the baseline, ③**swing** up to the midline, ④**down** to the baseline, ⑤**swing** up to the midline, ⑥**dip** connector at the midline. /w/

PRACTICE 1

i i i i i i i i i i

t t t t t t t t ✓

u u u u u u u u

s s s s s s s s

j j j j j j j j

p p p p p p p p

r r r r r r r

w w w w w w w w

CURVE LETTERS

Each of the lowercase curve letters begins on the baseline, curves up to the midline, and rolls back around to the baseline.

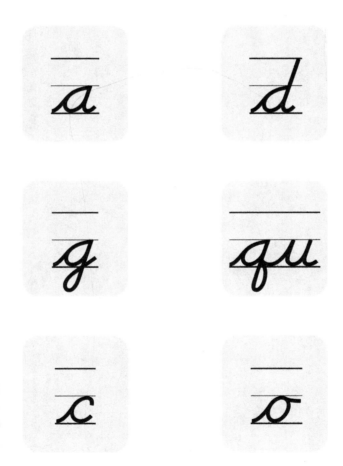

STROKES

CURVE

ROLL

SWING

DOWN

DROP-SWOOP

DROP-HOOK

DIP

①**Curve** up to the midline, ②**roll** back around to the baseline, ③**swing** up to the midline, ④**down** to the baseline.

/ă-ā-ä/

①**Curve** up to the midline, ②**roll** back around to the baseline, ③**swing tall** to the top line, ④slide **down** to the baseline.

/d/

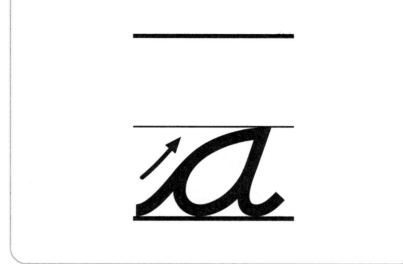

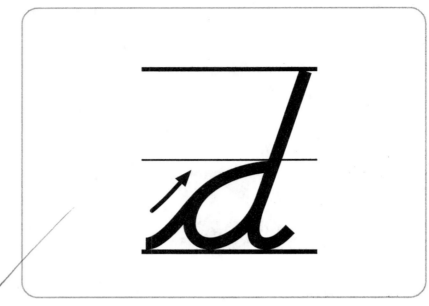

d d d d d d d

d d d d d d d

d

d

d

d

d

d

①**Curve** up to the midline, ②**roll** back around to the baseline, ③**swing** up to the midline, ④**drop** down halfway below the baseline, ⑤**swoop**.

/g-j/

①**Curve** up to the midline, ②**roll** back around to the baseline, ③**swing** up to the midline, ④**drop** down halfway below the baseline, ⑤**hook** up to the baseline, ⑥touch, ⑦**swing** up to the midline, ⑧**down** to the baseline, ⑨**swing** up to the midline, ⑩**down** to the baseline.

/kw/

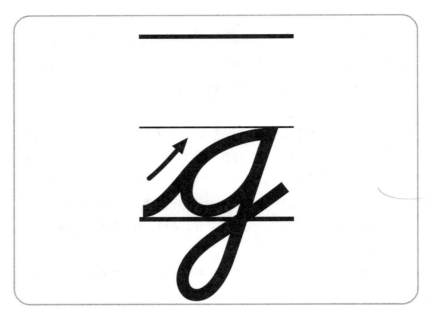

g g g g g g g g
g g g g g g g g g
g g g g g g g

g

g

g

g

g

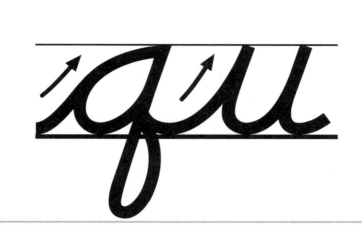

qu qu qu qu qu qu qu

qu qu qu qu qu qu qu

qu

qu

qu

qu

qu

qu

①**Curve** around to just below the midline, ②**roll** back around to just above the baseline.   /k-s/

①**Curve** around to just below the midline, ②**roll** back around past the baseline and up to the midline, ③**dip** connector at the midline.   /ŏ-ō-ö/

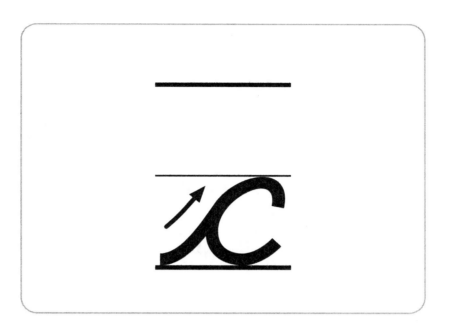

c c c c c c c

c c c c c c c

c

c

c

c

c

c

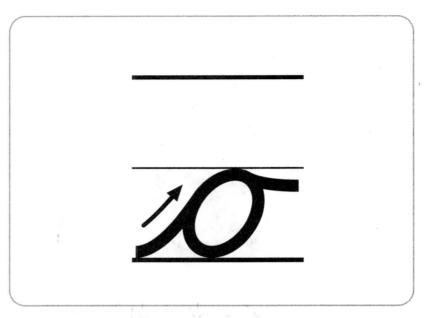

𝒐 𝒐 𝒐 𝒐 𝒐 𝒐 𝒐

𝒐 𝒐 𝒐 𝒐 𝒐 𝒐 𝒐

𝒐

𝒐

𝒐

𝒐

𝒐

𝒐

LETTERS THAT CONNECT AT THE BASELINE

Letters that end on the baseline connect from the baseline to the next letter. Read each word, then practice writing it with your pointer finger. Try to write each word with smooth, rhythmic motions. Finish writing all the connected letters in a word before crossing a t or dotting an i.

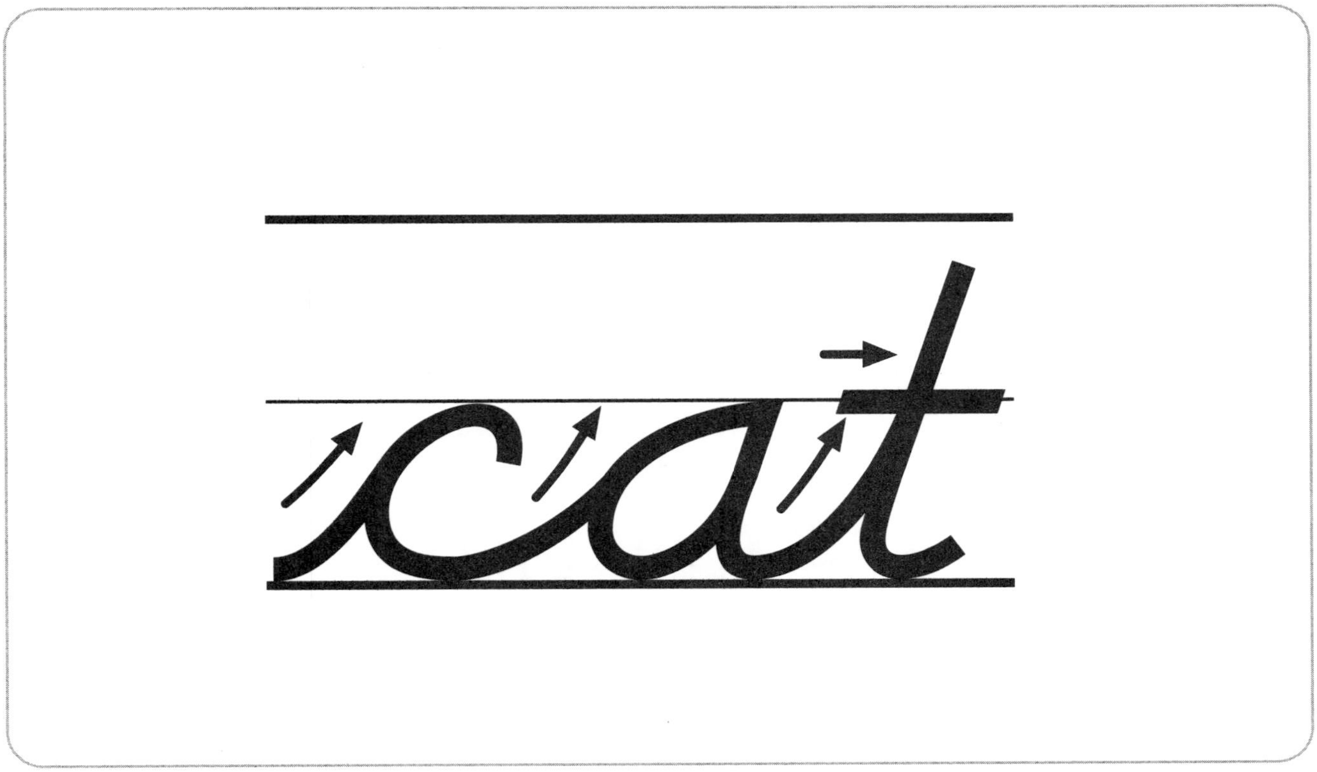
cat

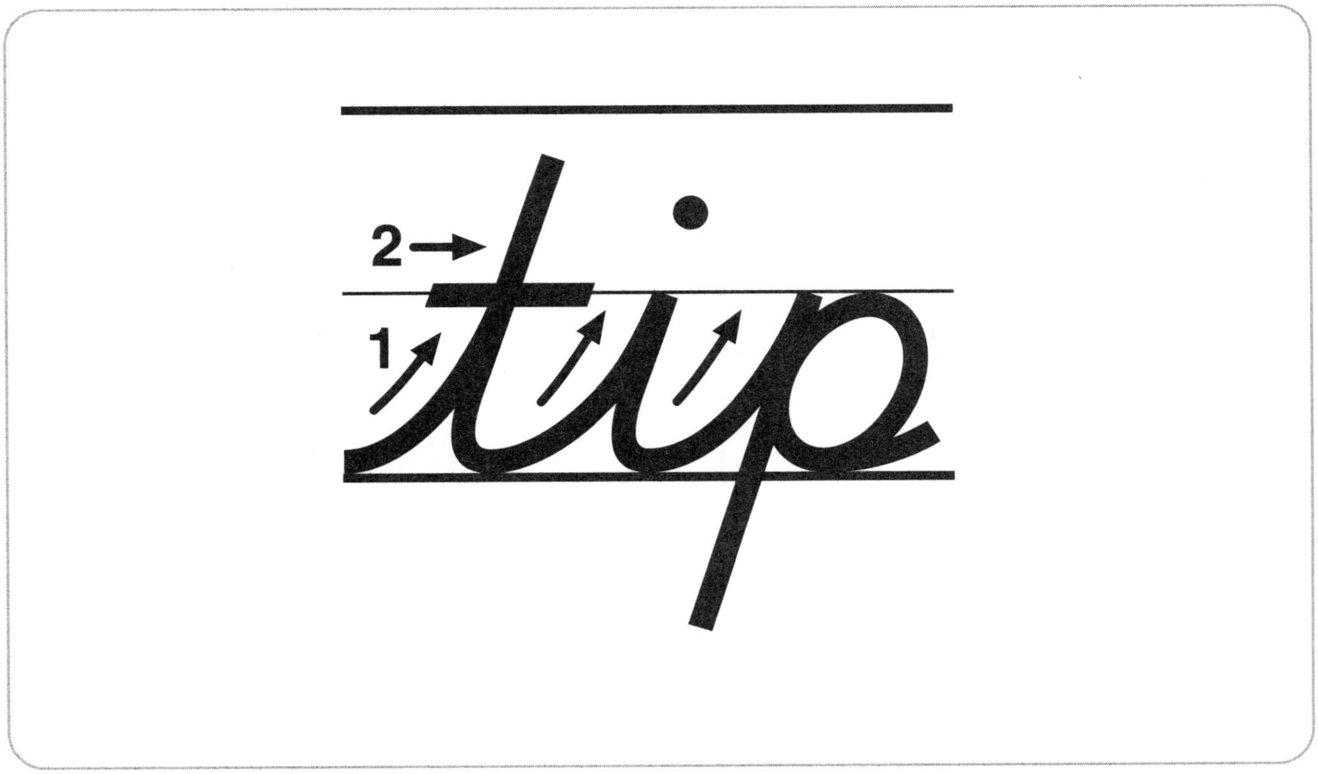
2
1
tip

PRACTICE 6

sat sat sat sat

us us us us

rip rip rip rip

sad sad sad sad

gap gap gap gap

rust rust rust rust

PRACTICE 7

dad dad dad dad

quit quit quit

pig pig pig

dip dip dip

jug jug jug

cut cut cut

PRACTICE 8

rug rug rug

act act act

gas gas gas

cup cup cup

it it it

drip drip drip

PRACTICE 9

dust dust dust

spit spit spit

rut rut rut

tip tip tip

at at at

pug pug pug

PRACTICE 10

did did did

tag tag tag

sit sit sit

rag rag rag

cat cat cat

just just just

LOOP LETTERS

Each of the lowercase loop letters begins on the baseline, loops up to the top line or the midline, and goes down toward the baseline.

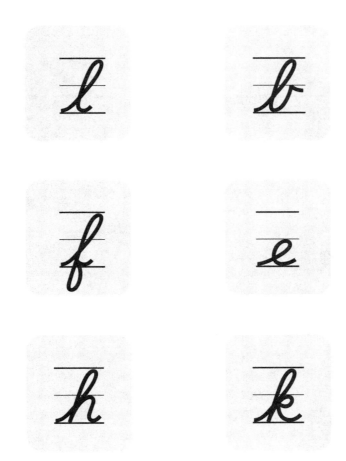

STROKES

LOOP

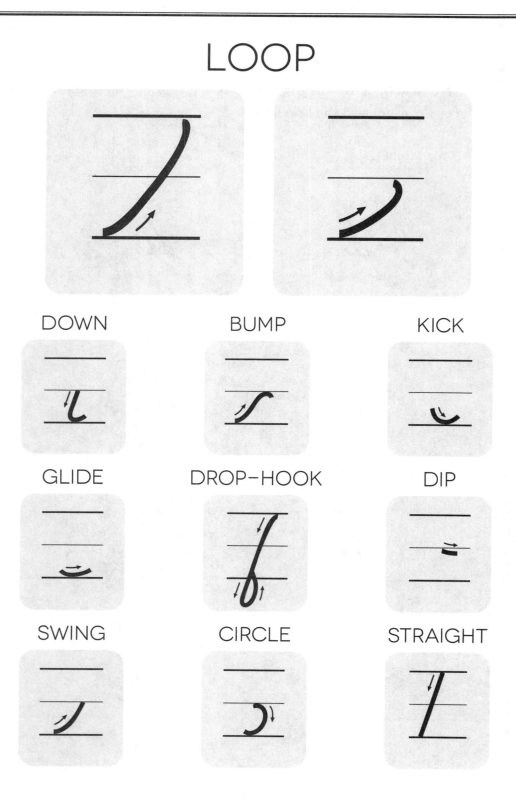

DOWN

BUMP

KICK

GLIDE

DROP-HOOK

DIP

SWING

CIRCLE

STRAIGHT

①**Loop** up to the top line, ②**down** to the baseline. /l/

①**Loop** up to the top line, ②**down** to the baseline, ③**swing** up to the midline, ④**dip** connector at the midline. /b/

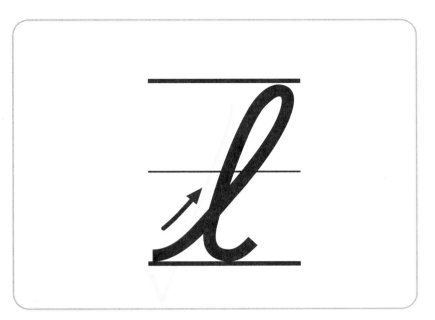

ℓ ℓℓℓℓℓℓ ℓ ℓ ℓ ℓ ℓ ℓ ℓ ℓ ℓ ℓℓℓℓ ℓ ℓ ℓ ℓ ℓ ℓ ℓℓℓ ℓ

ℓℓℓ ℓℓ ℓℓ ℓℓ ℓℓ ℓℓ ℓ ℓ ℓ ℓ ℓℓℓℓ ℓ

ℓ

ℓ

ℓ

ℓ

ℓ

ℓ

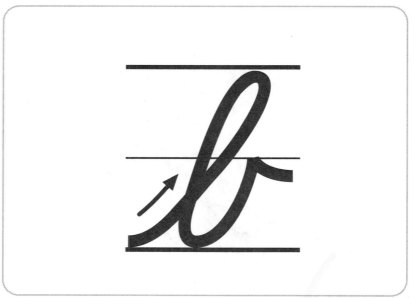

b b b b b b b b b b b b b b b b

b b b b b b b b b b b b b

b

b

b

b

b

b

f ①**Loop** up to the top line, ②**drop** down halfway below the baseline, ③**hook** up to the baseline, ④touch, ⑤**glide**.   /f/

e ①**Small loop** up to the midline, ②**down** to the baseline.   /ĕ-ē/

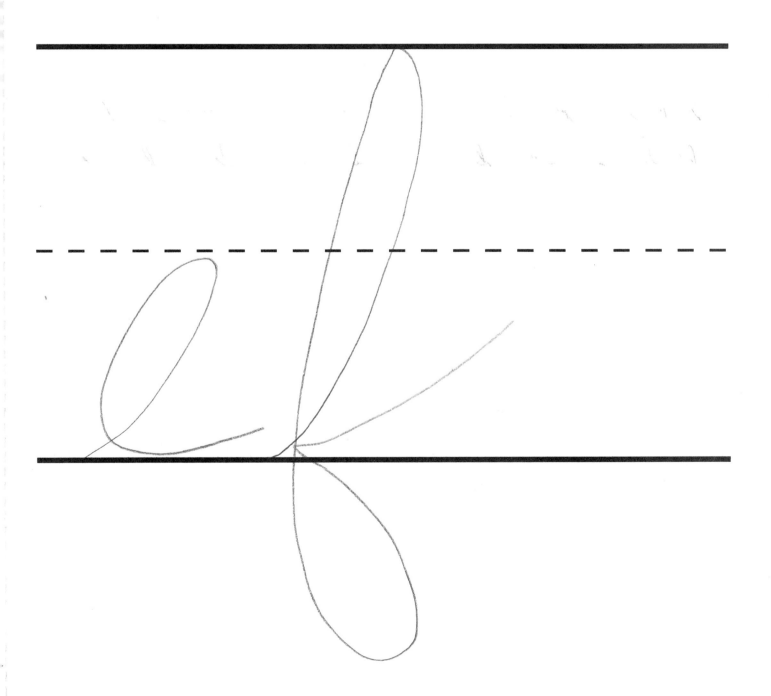

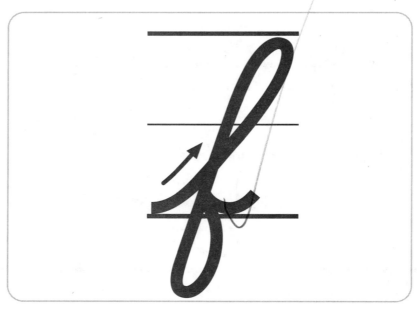

$\mathcal{e}$ $\mathcal{e}$ $\mathcal{e}$ $\mathcal{e}$ $\mathcal{e}$ $\mathcal{e}$ $\mathcal{e}$ $\mathcal{e}$ $\mathcal{e}$ $\mathcal{e}$ $\mathcal{e}$ $\mathcal{e}$ $\mathcal{e}$ $\mathcal{e}$ $\mathcal{e}$ $\mathcal{e}$ $\mathcal{e}$

$\mathcal{e}$ $\mathcal{e}$ $\mathcal{e}$ $\mathcal{e}$ $\mathcal{e}$ $\mathcal{e}$ $\mathcal{e}$ $\mathcal{e}$ $\mathcal{e}$ $\mathcal{e}$ $\mathcal{e}$ $\mathcal{e}$ $\mathcal{e}$ $\mathcal{e}$ $\mathcal{e}$

$\mathcal{e}$ $\mathcal{e}$ $\mathcal{e}$ $\mathcal{e}$ $\mathcal{e}$ $\mathcal{e}$ $\mathcal{e}$ $\mathcal{e}$ $\mathcal{e}$ $\mathcal{e}$ $\mathcal{e}$ $\mathcal{e}$ $\mathcal{e}$ $\mathcal{e}$

$\mathcal{e}$ $\mathcal{e}$ $\mathcal{e}$ $\mathcal{e}$ $\mathcal{e}$ $\mathcal{e}$ $\mathcal{e}$ $\mathcal{e}$ $\mathcal{e}$ $\mathcal{e}$ $\mathcal{e}$ $\mathcal{e}$ $\mathcal{e}$

$\mathcal{e}$

$\mathcal{e}$

$\mathcal{e}$

$\mathcal{e}$

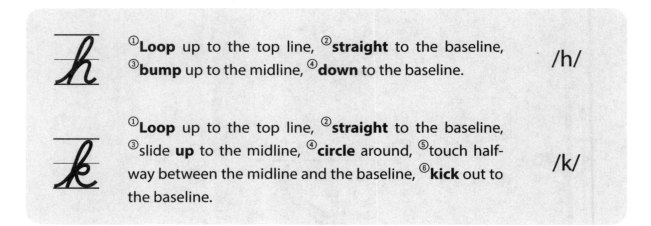

①**Loop** up to the top line, ②**straight** to the baseline, ③**bump** up to the midline, ④**down** to the baseline.

/h/

①**Loop** up to the top line, ②**straight** to the baseline, ③slide **up** to the midline, ④**circle** around, ⑤**touch** half-way between the midline and the baseline, ⑥**kick** out to the baseline.

/k/

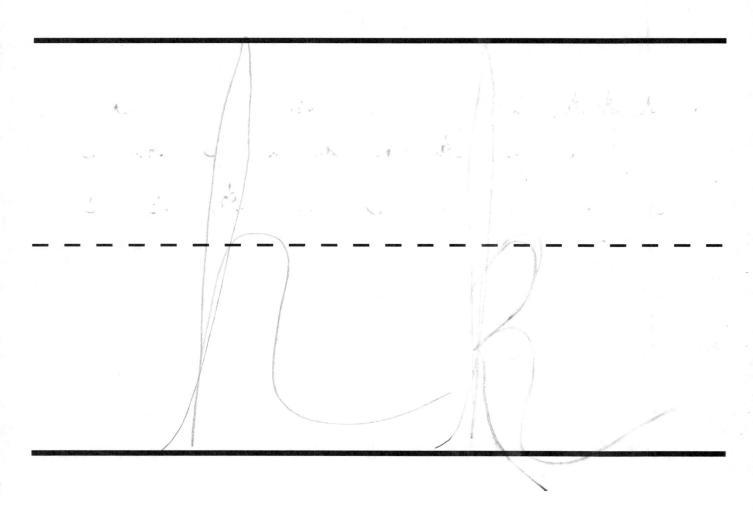

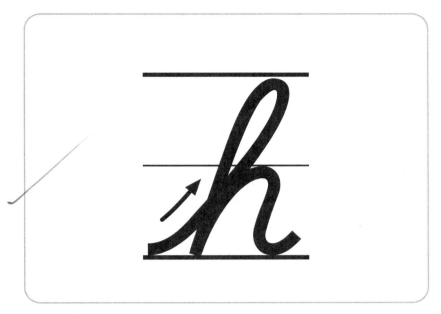

h h h h h h h h h h h h h h
h h h h h h h h h h h h h h
h h h h h h h h h h h h h h
h h h h h h h h h h h h h h

h

h

h

h

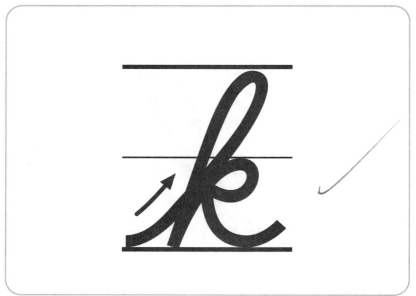

k k k k k k k k k k k k
k k k k k k k k k k k k
k k k k k k k k k k k k
k
k
k
k
k

PRACTICE 11

l

b

f

e

h

k

a

g

o

qu

c

p

PRACTICE 12

d

l

g

qu

c

b

o

f

h

k

e

r

PRACTICE 13

l

b

f

e

h

k

a

d

g

qu

c

o

PRACTICE 14

had

cub

stuff

glad

hid

tell

PRACTICE 15

lab

fill

kiss

help

lid

kept

PRACTICE 16

last

frisk

grab

kid

hat

quest

LETTERS THAT CONNECT WITH A DIP CONNECTOR

Letters that end with a dip connector connect to the next letter just below the midline. Notice how the dip connector does not change the size of the following letter. Rather, the next letter begins near the midline. Read each word, then practice writing it with your pointer finger. Try to write each word with smooth, rhythmic motions. Finish writing all the connected letters in a word before crossing a t or dotting an i.

wet bug

bad fog

PRACTICE 17

top

best

wag

rod

kit

wet

PRACTICE 18

west

pop

bed

fog

well

hug

PRACTICE 19

cot

bag

stop

frog

bell

will

PRACTICE 20

last bus

best list

hot jog

glad dog

wet wig

big boss

PRACTICE 21

left bag

wag fast

bell top

big craft

pop it

cut sod

BUMP LETTERS

Each of the lowercase bump letters begins on the baseline and bumps up to the midline.

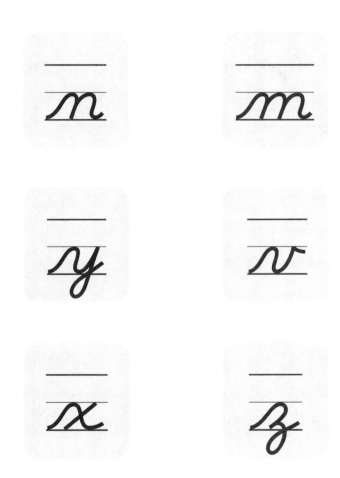

STROKES

BUMP

STRAIGHT   SWING   DROP-SWOOP

SLASH   KICK   TUCK

DOWN   DIP

①**Bump** up to the midline, ②**straight** to the baseline, ③**bump** up to the midline, ④**down**.   /n/

①**Bump** up to the midline, ②**straight** to the baseline, ③**bump** up to the midline, ④**straight** to the baseline, ⑤**bump** up to the midline, ⑥**down**.   /m/

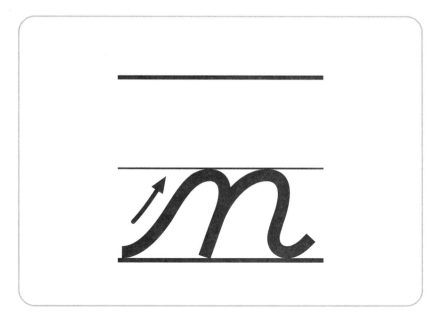

n n n n n n n n n n n n n n n n n n n

n n n n n n n n n n n n n n n n n n n

n n n n n n n n n n n n n n n n n n n

n n n n n n n n n n n n n n n n n n n

n

n

n

n

m m m m m m m m m m m m m m m

m m m m m m m m m m m m m m m

m m m m m m m m m m m m m m m

m m m m m m m m m m m m m m m

m

m

m

m

①**Bump** up to the midline, ②**down** to the baseline, ③**swing** up to the midline, ④**drop** down halfway below the baseline, ⑤**swoop**.   /y-ĭ-ī-ē/

①**Bump** up to the midline, ②**down** to the baseline, ③**swing** up to the midline, ④**dip** connector at the midline.   /v/

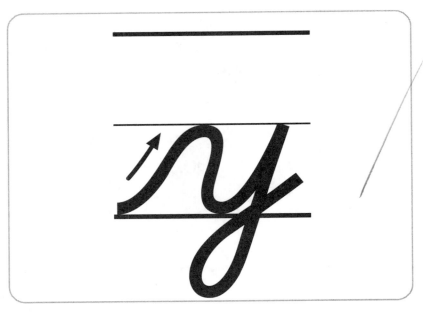

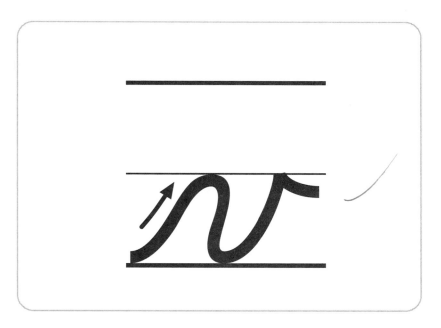

①**Bump** up to the midline, ②**kick** down to the baseline, ③pick up the pencil, start at the midline, ④**slash** down to the baseline.

/ks-z/

①**Bump** up to the midline, ②**tuck** down to the baseline, ③**drop** down halfway below the baseline, ④**swoop**.

/z/

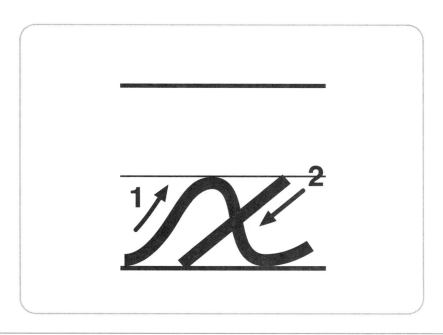

x

x

x

x

x

x

x

x

PRACTICE 22

n

m

y

v

x

z

h

b

f

k

qu

j

PRACTICE 23

d

n

g

m

c

l

v

e

x

a

z

y

PRACTICE 24

x

n

o

y

h

k

z

d

g

v

b

m

PRACTICE 25

yes it can

man will win

vent flap

zip it up

hint hint

get on jet

Practice 26

land at flag

flip a map

jam and eggs

fix van

cliff jump

zap bugs

PRACTICE 27

not eggs

yum yum

twin drums

vast sand

pink cast

slim man

Practice 28

blend tints

not wet yet

pink vest

mop mess

fan can run

soft quilt

PRACTICE 29

bugs buzz

drum set

just a bump

fox hunt

hen struts

tan cap

PRACTICE 30

get a job

stand up

step on

big box

frost it

sat in dust

Uppercase
Cursive LETTERS

CURVE LETTERS

Each of the uppercase curve letters begins halfway between the midline and the top line and curves up toward the top line.

$\mathcal{P}$ $\mathcal{B}$ $\mathcal{R}$

$\mathcal{N}$ $\mathcal{M}$ $\mathcal{K}$

$\mathcal{H}$ $\mathcal{U}$ $\mathcal{Y}$

$\mathcal{W}$ $\mathcal{V}$

$\mathcal{X}$ $\mathcal{Z}$

STROKES

CURVE

STRAIGHT

CIRCLE

UP

GLIDE

KICK

BUMP

DOWN

SLASH

SLASH

SWIRL

SWING

DROP-SWOOP

DIP

TUCK

Start halfway between the midline and the top line. ①**Curve** up to the top line, ②**straight** to the baseline, ③slide **up** to the top line, ④**circle** around to the midline.

Start halfway between the midline and the top line. ①**Curve** up to the top line, ②**straight** to the baseline, ③slide **up** to the top line, ④**circle** around to the midline, ⑤**circle** around past the baseline, ⑥touch, ⑦**glide** across.

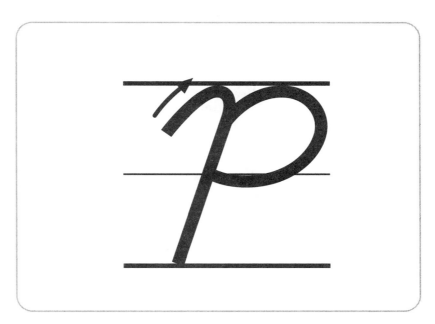

$\mathcal{P}$

$\mathcal{P}$

$\mathcal{P}$

$\mathcal{P}$

$\mathcal{P}$

$\mathcal{P}$

$\mathcal{P}$

$\mathcal{P}$

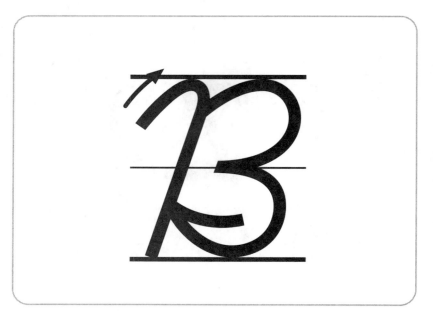

Start halfway between the midline and the top line. [1]**Curve** up to the top line, [2]**straight** to the baseline, [3]slide **up** to the top line, [4]**circle** around to the midline, [5]touch, [6]**kick** down to the baseline.

Start halfway between the midline and the top line. [1]**Curve** up to the top line, [2]**straight** to the baseline, [3]**bump** up to the top line, [4]**down**.

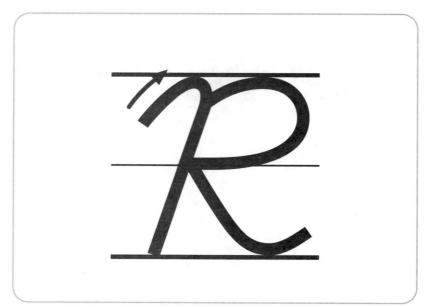

R

R

R

R

R

R

R

R

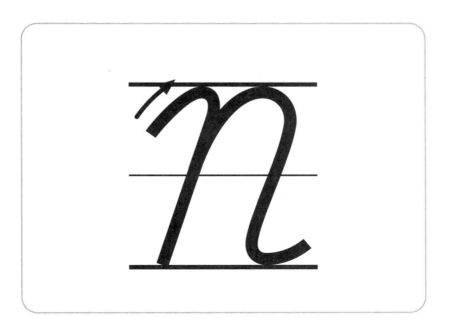

n

n

n

n

n

n

n

n

Start halfway between the midline and the top line. [1]**Curve** up to the top line, [2]**straight** to the baseline, [3]**bump** up to the top line, [4]**straight** to the baseline, [5]**bump** up to the top line, [6]**down**.

Start halfway between the midline and the top line. [1]**Curve** up to the top line, [2]**straight** to the baseline, [3]pick up the pencil, start at the top line, [4]**slash** down to the midline, [5]**kick** down to the baseline.

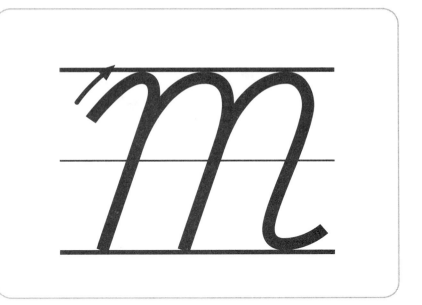

m

m

m

m

m

m

m

m

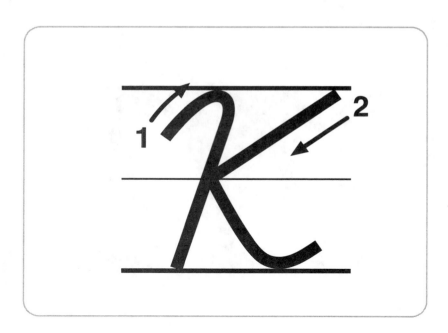

$\mathcal{K}$

$\mathcal{K}$

$\mathcal{K}$

$\mathcal{K}$

$\mathcal{K}$

$\mathcal{K}$

$\mathcal{K}$

$\mathcal{K}$

Start halfway between the midline and the top line. ①**Curve** up to the top line, ②**straight** to the baseline, ③pick up the pencil, start at the top line, ④**straight** to the baseline, ⑤slide **up** to the midline, ⑥**swirl**.

Start halfway between the midline and the top line. ①**Curve** up to the top line, ②**down** to the baseline, ③**swing** up to the top line, ④**down** to the baseline.

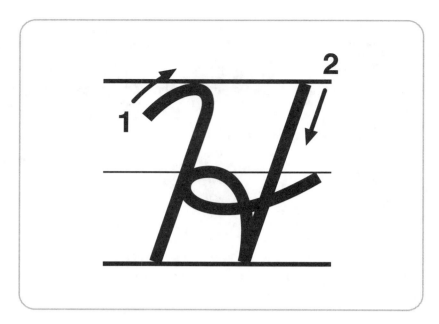

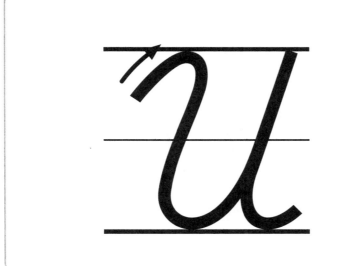

$\mathcal{U}$

$\mathcal{U}$

$\mathcal{U}$

$\mathcal{U}$

$\mathcal{U}$

$\mathcal{U}$

$\mathcal{U}$

$\mathcal{U}$

Start halfway between the midline and the top line. ①**Curve** up to the top line, ②**down** to the baseline, ③**swing** up to the top line, ④**drop** down halfway below the baseline, ⑤**swoop**.

Start halfway between the midline and the top line. ①**Curve** up to the top line, ②**down** to the baseline, ③**swing** up to the top line, ④**down** to the baseline, ⑤**swing** up to the top line, ⑥**dip** below the top line.

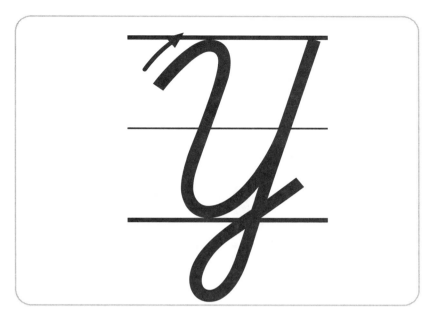

𝒴

𝒴

𝒴

𝒴

𝒴

𝒴

𝒴

𝒴

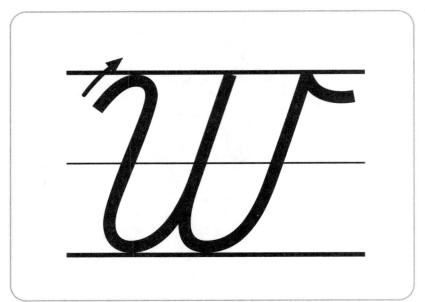

w

w

w

w

w

w

w

w

Start halfway between the midline and the top line. ①**Curve** up to the top line, ②**down** to the baseline, ③**swing** up to the top line, ④**dip** just below the top line.

Start halfway between the midline and the top line. ①**Curve** up to the top line, ②**kick** down to the baseline, ③pick up the pencil, start at the top line, ④**slash** down to the baseline.

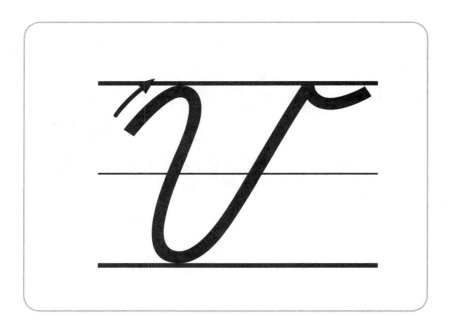

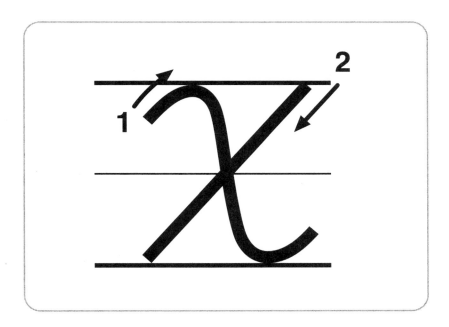

x
x
x
x
x
x
x
x

Start halfway between the midline and the top line. ①**Curve** up to the top line, ②**tuck** down to the baseline, ③**drop** down halfway below the baseline, ④**swoop**.

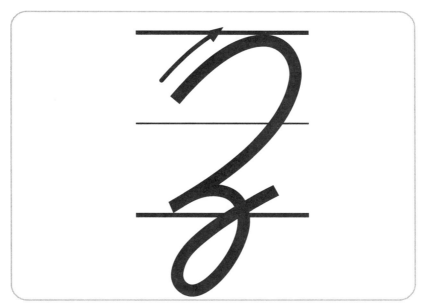

PRACTICE 31

B

R

n

m

K

H

U

Y

W

V

X

Z

Practice 32

X

W

B

n

m

K

R

H

U

Y

Z

P

PRACTICE 33

V

P

Y

H

X

n

Z

m

W

K

U

B

Uppercase Letters That Connect At The Baseline

Uppercase letters that end on the baseline connect from the baseline to the second letter within the word. Read each word, then practice writing it with your pointer finger. Try to write each word with smooth, rhythmic motions. Finish writing all the connected letters in a word before crossing a t or dotting an i.

Run

Yes

PRACTICE 34

Up

Us

Ran

Rest

Ken

Kris

Practice 35

Nests

Nap

Men

Mops

Rob

Meg

PRACTICE 36

Yes

Yams

Zip

Zag

Next

Until

Uppercase Letters
That Do Not Connect

When an uppercase letter does not end on the baseline it is not connected to the following letters. Pick up the pencil and begin the second letter of the word on the baseline. Try to write each word with smooth, rhythmic motions. Finish writing all the connected letters in a word before crossing a t or dotting an i.

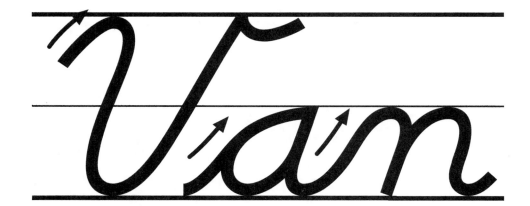

Wet

Hug

Pal

Bag

PRACTICE 37

Big

Blink

Pal

Print

Hot

Hiss

PRACTICE 38

Wet

Will

Van

Vent

Hand

Belt

PRACTICE 39

Brag

Wigs

Vets

Prank

Hint

Vest

ROLL LETTERS

Each of the uppercase roll letters begins on or just below the top line and rolls toward the midline or baseline.

STROKES

ROLL

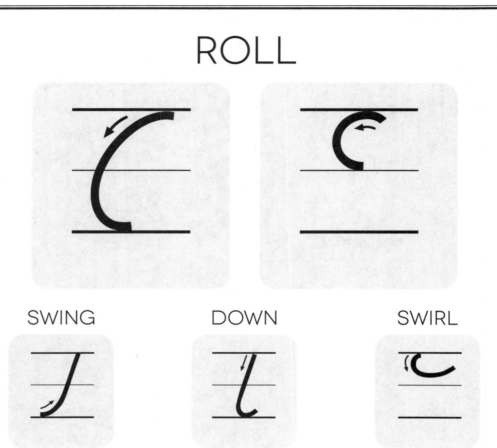

SWING   DOWN   SWIRL

Start at the top line. ①**Roll** around to the baseline, ②**swing** up to the top line, ③**down** to the baseline.

 Start at the top line. ①**Roll** around past the baseline and back up to the top line, ②**swirl**.

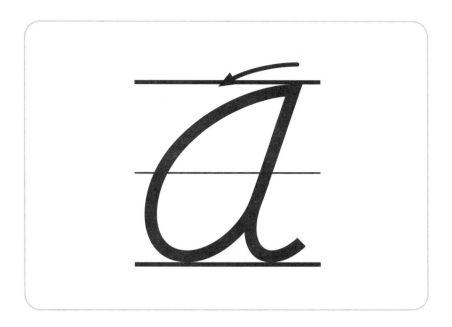

a

a

a

a

a

a

a

a

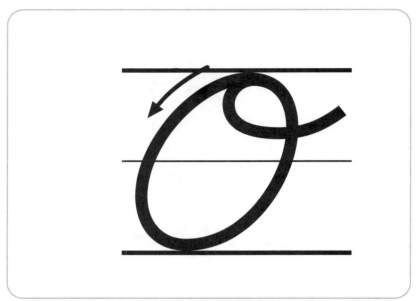

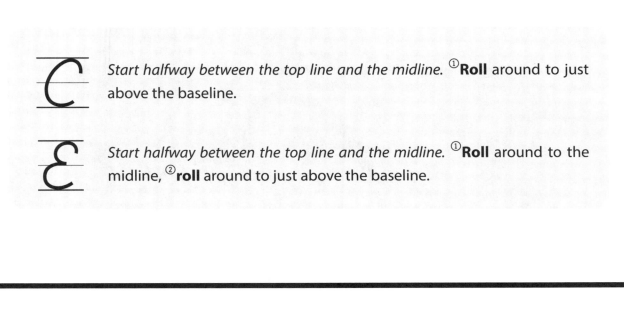

Start halfway between the top line and the midline. [1]**Roll** around to just above the baseline.

Start halfway between the top line and the midline. [1]**Roll** around to the midline, [2]**roll** around to just above the baseline.

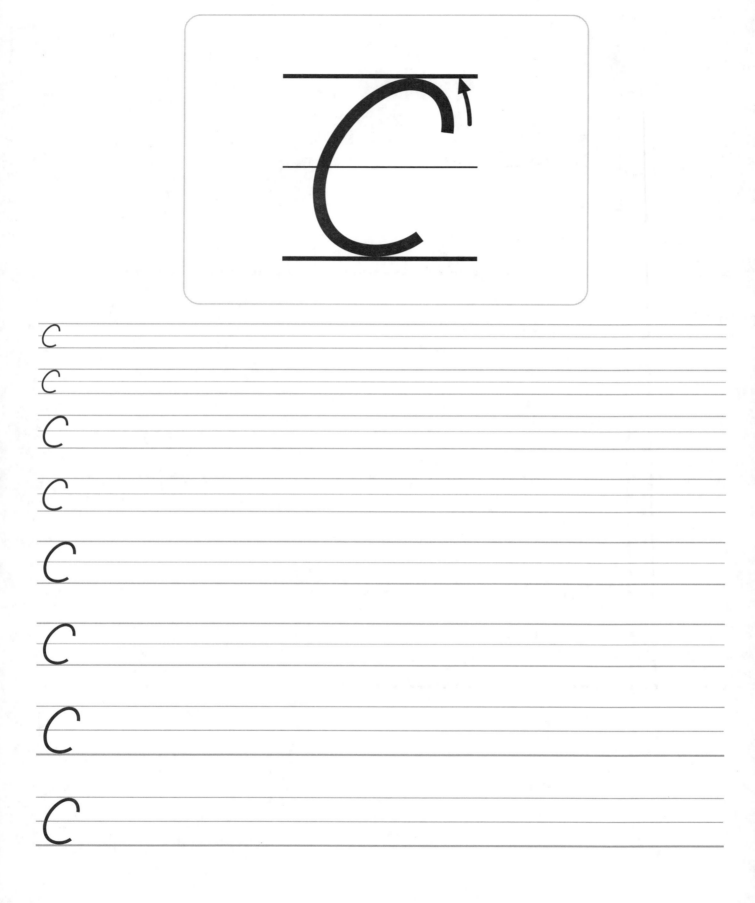

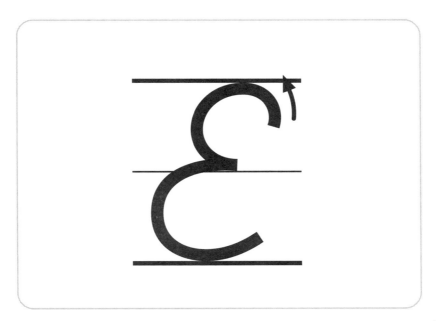

Ɛ

Ɛ

Ɛ

Ɛ

Ɛ

Ɛ

Ɛ

Ɛ

PRACTICE 40

A

O

C

E

X

Z

N

B

Y

K

W

H

Practice 41

Ant

At

And

On

Oxen

Off

PRACTICE 42

Cat

Cap

Can

Egg

End

Ebb

LOOP LETTERS

Each of the uppercase loop letters begins on the baseline, loops up to the top line, and goes down to the midline.

STROKES

LOOP

DOWN

SWING

GLIDE

SCOOP

Start at the baseline. ①**Loop** up to the top line, ②**down** to the midline, ③**swing** up to halfway between the midline and the top line, ④**scoop** around past the baseline, ⑤**glide** across.

 Start at the baseline. ①**Loop** up to the top line, ②**down** to the midline, ③**scoop** around past the baseline, ④**glide** across.

Practice 43

Get

Gap

Glad

Stand

Step

Send

PRACTICE 44

Grass

Swim

Pen

Went

Bond

Nod

CIRCLE LETTERS

Each of the uppercase circle letters begins on the baseline and circles up to the top line.

STROKES

CIRCLE

DROP–SWOOP

LOOP

Start at the baseline. ①Tight **circle** around to the top line, ②**drop** down halfway below the baseline, ③**swoop**.

 Start at the baseline. ①**Circle** around past the top line to the baseline, ②**loop** on the baseline.

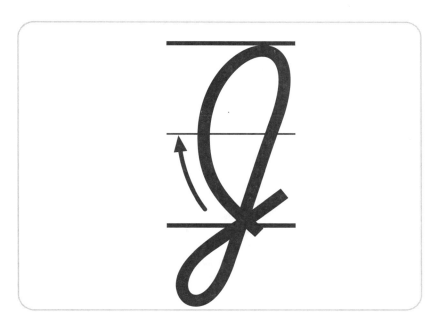

Q

Q

Q

Q

Q

Q

Q

Q

PRACTICE 45

Job

Jam

Jog

Queen

Quit

Quilt

PRACTICE 46

Jess

Quip

Hiss

Set

Alan

Ron

SLASH LETTERS

Each of the uppercase slash letters begins near the top line and slashes toward the baseline.

STROKES

SLASH

SCOOP

CROSS

ROLL

GLIDE

LOOP

SWIRL

SWERVE

Start just below the top line. ①**Slash** down to the baseline, ②**scoop** up to halfway between the baseline and the midline, ③**glide** across, ④pick up the pencil, ⑤**swerve** at the top.

Start just below the top line. ①**Slash** down to the baseline, ②**scoop** up to halfway between the baseline and the midline, ③**glide** across, ④pick up the pencil, ⑤**swerve** at the top, ⑥pick up the pencil, ⑦**cross** at the midline.

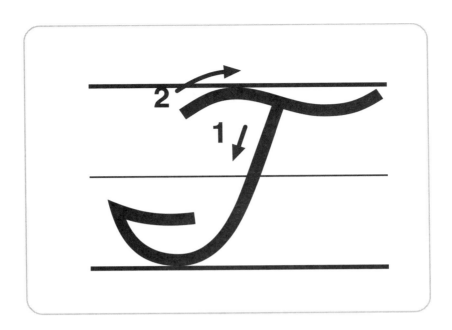

$\mathcal{T}$

$\mathcal{T}$

$\mathcal{T}$

$\mathcal{T}$

$\mathcal{T}$

$\mathcal{T}$

$\mathcal{T}$

$\mathcal{T}$

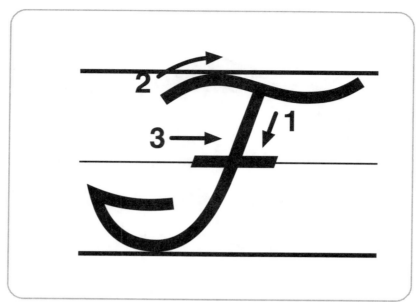

Start just below the top line. [1]**Slash** down past the midline, [2]**loop** on the baseline, [3]**roll** to the top line, [4]**swirl**.

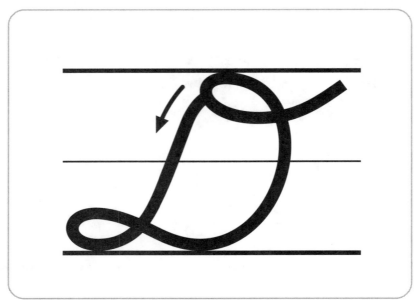

PRACTICE 47

$\mathcal{T}$

$\mathcal{F}$

$\mathcal{D}$

$\mathcal{E}$

$\mathcal{X}$

$\mathcal{Z}$

$\mathcal{M}$

$\mathcal{O}$

$\mathcal{U}$

$\mathcal{Y}$

$\mathcal{V}$

$\mathcal{H}$

PRACTICE 48

Tents

Tap

Trips

Frost

Fun

Dad

Dogs

PRACTICE 49

Dan

Fred

Ted

Sam

Will

Ken

PRACTICE 50

Mill

Trunk

Act

Rust

Fix

Him

Desk

MISCELLANEOUS LETTERS

Each of the miscellaneous uppercase letters begins with a different initial stroke.

STROKES

MISCELLANEOUS

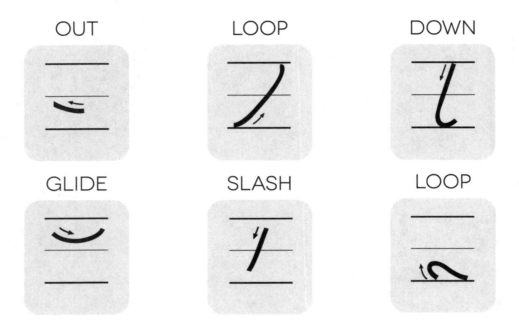

OUT	LOOP	DOWN

GLIDE	SLASH	LOOP

Start halfway between the baseline and the midline. ①**Out**, ②roll down to the baseline, ③**loop** up to the top line, ④**down** to the baseline.

Start halfway between the midline and the top line. ①**Glide** up to the top line, ②roll, ③**slash** down to the baseline, ④**loop** on the baseline.

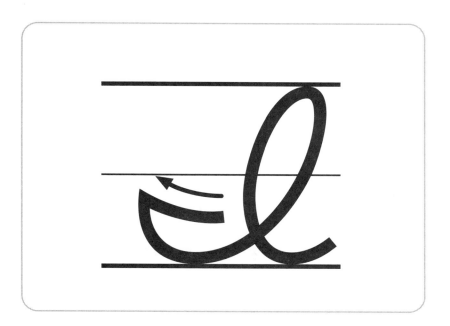

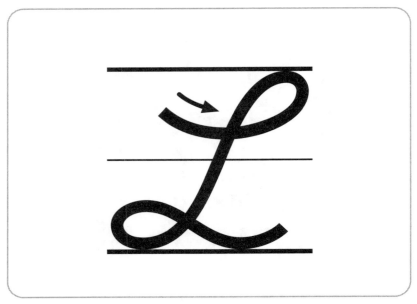

$\mathscr{L}$

$\mathscr{L}$

$\mathscr{L}$

$\mathscr{L}$

$\mathscr{L}$

$\mathscr{L}$

$\mathscr{L}$

$\mathscr{L}$

PRACTICE 51

If

In

It

Land

Limp

Logs

Practice 52

Twin

Lost

Gasp

Melt

Ink

Pump

PRACTICE 53

Zest

Silt

Bunk

Cost

Left

Fond

PRACTICE 54

Ask

Buzz

Crisp

Doll

Elf

Fist

Gift

Help

It

Jan

Kept

Left

Map

Nuts

Often

Plunk

Quilt

Rex

Self

Tag

Us

Vans

West

Yaks

Zap

NUMBERS

Numbers are written the same in both cursive and manuscript handwriting.

1   2   3

4   5   6

7   8   9

0

STROKES

NUMBERS

STRAIGHT

CIRCLE

ROLL

CROSS

CIRCLE

ROLL

CURVE

ANGLE UP

ROLL

SLASH

SWING

ROLL

Start at the top line. ①**Straight** to the baseline.

Start halfway between the top line and the midline. ①**Circle** around to the midline, ②**slash** down to the baseline, ③**cross** at the baseline.

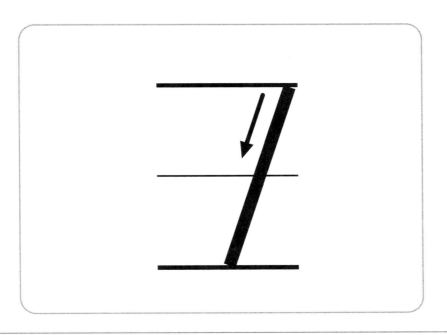

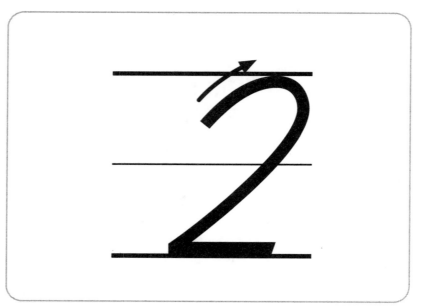

2

2

2

2

2

2

2

2

3 *Start just below the top line.* ①**Circle** around to the midline, ②**circle** around past the baseline.

4 *Start at the top line.* ①**Straight** to the midline, ②**cross** at the midline, ③pick up the pencil, start at the top line, ④**straight** to the baseline.

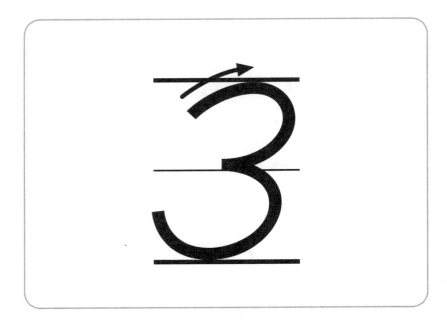

3

3

3

3

3

3

3

3

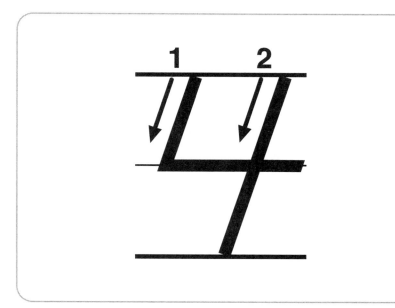

5 *Start at the top line.* ①**Cross** to the left at the top line, ②**straight** to the midline, ③**circle** around past the baseline.

6 *Start at the top line.* ①**Slash** down to halfway between the midline and the baseline, ②**roll** around past the baseline, back up past the midline, ③touch.

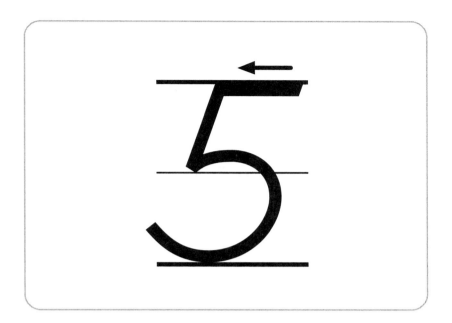

5
5
5
5
5
5
5
5

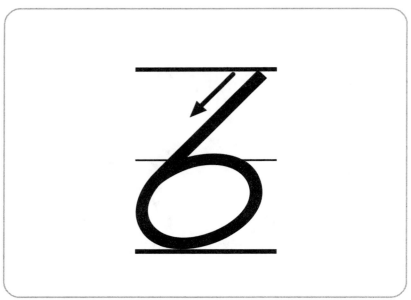

6

6

6

6

6

6

6

6

Z *Start at the top line.* ①**Cross** at the top line, ②**slash** down to the baseline.

8 *Start just below the top line.* ①**Roll** around to the midline, ②**curve** back past the baseline, ③**angle up** to the top line.

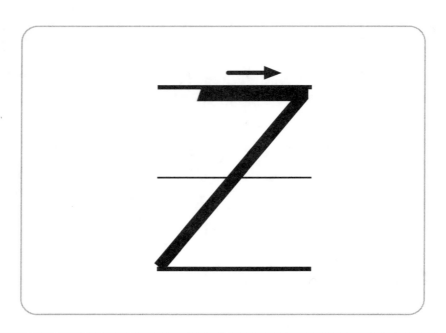

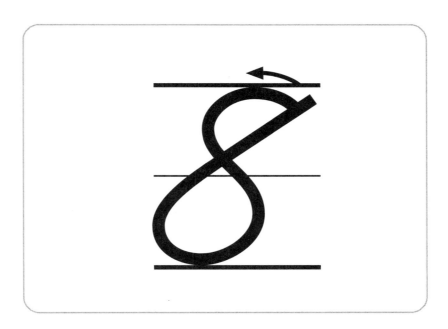

8

8

8

8

8

8

8

8

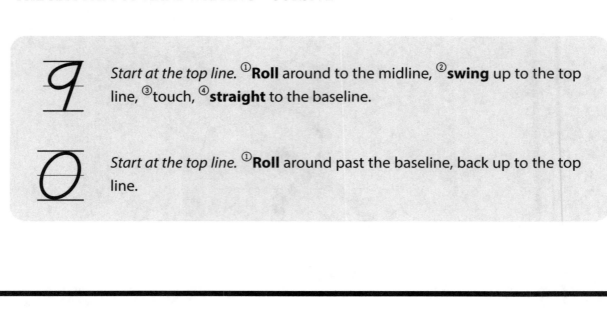

Start at the top line. ①**Roll** around to the midline, ②**swing** up to the top line, ③touch, ④**straight** to the baseline.

Start at the top line. ①**Roll** around past the baseline, back up to the top line.

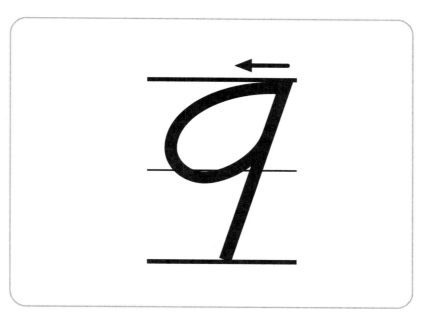

q

q

q

q

q

q

q

q

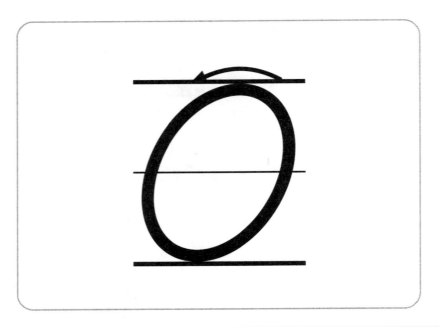

Practice 55

0

1

2

3

4

5

6

7

8

9

10

PRACTICE 56

11

12

13

14

15

16

17

18

19

20

PRACTICE 57

0

zero

1

one

2

two

3

three

4

four

5

five

PRACTICE 58

6

six

7

seven

8

eight

9

nine

10

ten

11

eleven

PRACTICE 59

12

twelve

13

thirteen

14

fourteen

15

fifteen

16

sixteen

17

seventeen

PRACTICE 60

18

eighteen

19

nineteen

20

twenty

100

one hundred

1,000

one thousand

1,000,000

one million